W9-CRV-503

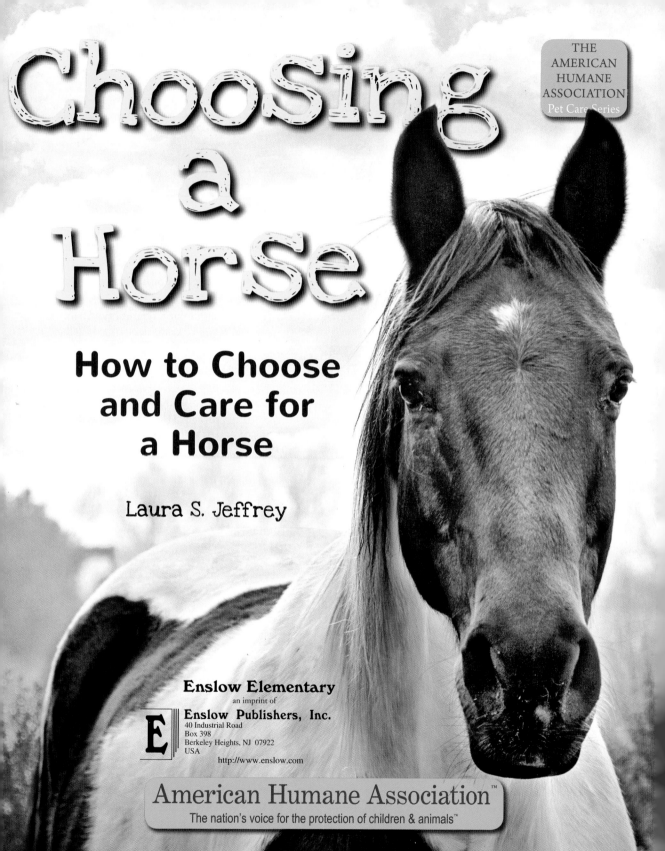

Choosing a Horse

How to Choose and Care for a Horse

Laura S. Jeffrey

Enslow Elementary
an imprint of
Enslow Publishers, Inc.
40 Industrial Road
Box 398
Berkeley Heights, NJ 07922
USA

http://www.enslow.com

American Humane Association™
The nation's voice for the protection of children & animals™

American Humane Association™
The nation's voice for the protection of children & animals™

Since 1877, American Humane Association has been at the forefront of virtually every major advance in protecting children, pets, and farm animals from cruelty, abuse, and neglect. Today we're also leading the way in understanding the human-animal bond and its role in therapy, medicine, and society. American Humane Association reaches millions of people every day through groundbreaking research, education, training, and services that span a wide network of organizations, agencies, and businesses. You can help make a difference, too. Visit www.americanhumane.org today, call 1-866-242-1877, or write to American Humane Association at 1400 16th Street NW, Suite 360, Washington, DC 20036.

Enslow Elementary, an imprint of Enslow Publishers, Inc.

Enslow Elementary® is a registered trademark of Enslow Publishers, Inc.

Copyright © 2013 by Enslow Publishers, Inc.

All rights reserved.

No part of this book may be reproduced by any means without the written permission of the publisher.

Library of Congress Cataloging-in-Publication Data
Jeffrey, Laura S.
  Choosing a horse : how to choose and care for a horse / Laura S. Jeffrey.
    p. cm. — (The American Humane Association pet care series)
  Includes bibliographical references and index.
  Summary: "Discusses the selection, housing, diet, handling, grooming, and health of a new horse"— Provided by publisher.
  ISBN 978-0-7660-4083-0
  1. Horses—Juvenile literature. 2. Horsemanship—Juvenile literature. I. Title.
  SF302.J458 2013
  636.1—dc23
                                    2011049141

Future Editions:
Paperback ISBN 978-1-4644-0218-0
ePUB ISBN 978-1-4645-1131-8
PDF ISBN 978-1-4646-1131-5

Printed in the United States of America

082012 Lake Book Manufacturing, Inc., Melrose Park, IL

10 9 8 7 6 5 4 3 2 1

Photo Credits: Achim Prill/Photos.com, p. 11; AP Images, p. 9; Blair Seitz/Photo Researchers, Inc., p. 43; Claudia Steininger/Photos.com, p. 44 (bottom); Craig Barhorst/Photos.com, p. 40; David R. Frazier/Photo Researchers, Inc., p. 38; Eric Isselée/Photos.com, pp. 19, 22, 30; Henry Smith/Photos.com, p. 33; © iStockphoto.com/Francisco Romero, p. 14; © iStockphoto.com/Robert Churchill, p. 15; © iStockphoto.com/Rosalind Morgan, p. 44 (top); Jeffrey Banke/Photos.com, p. 29; Jupiterimages/Photos.com, pp. 6, 27; Karen Givens/Photos.com, p. 34; Magdalena Marczewska/Photos.com, p. 36; Mikhail Kondrashov/Photos.com, p. 23; pimmimemom/Photos.com, p. 25; Pontus Edenberg/Photos.com, p. 17; Shutterstock.com, pp. 4, 5, 7, 10, 16, 18, 21, 28, 31, 35, 39, 41, 45; Svetlana Mihailova/Photos.com, p. 42; Viktoria Makarova/Photos.com, p. 13. **Cover Photo:** Shutterstock.com (brown and white paint horse).

Table of Contents

Chapter 1

Great Pets

Horses are symbols of grace, freedom, and speed with their flowing manes and majestic bodies. It is no wonder that so many people want a horse for a pet.

Horses can be very challenging to take care of, however. Owning a horse means more than providing a pasture, a bucket of water, and some feed.

An Appaloosa horse

Horses are strong and powerful animals.

Horses need regular grooming and daily exercise. They need to eat special food, and their hooves require regular care. They need constant company throughout their entire life.

This book will help you choose a horse for a pet. It will tell you what to feed your new pet and how to make it feel comfortable and safe. This book will help you to know about keeping your horse healthy and happy.

While very beautiful, horses can be difficult to take care of. They need care every day.

Chapter 2

The History of Horses

Horses have a long and important history in the world. They are believed to have come from Asia somewhere around 3000 or 4000 B.C. Early Spanish explorers brought horses to North America. Horses quickly became popular with American Indians.

Before cars or planes were invented, horses were used to carry people and goods.

In ancient times, horses were used to pull carts and wagons.

Because of their great speed and strength, horses were used in wartime to carry soldiers to battle. Later, they were used by armies to carry heavy loads. Horses pulled wagons and supplies.

The first miniature horses came from Europe in the 1500s. Kings and wealthy people kept them as pets. English farmers used them for chores. In the 1800s, miniature ponies helped to pull coal out of mines. By the 1900s, equipment powered by electricity replaced the horses, and horses became pets.

Some horses became famous. During the Civil War (1861–1865), General Robert E. Lee had a horse named Traveller. They were together for many years. After Lee died, Traveller walked behind the wagon that carried Lee's body during the funeral procession. Traveller is now buried outside the entrance of the museum of Washington and Lee University in Virginia.

Seabiscuit is another famous horse. Seabiscuit was a racehorse during the Great Depression, in the 1930s. Whenever Seabiscuit raced, thousands of Americans traveled to watch him. Others listened to the race action on the radio.

The famous racehorse Seabiscuit has his picture taken before a race in 1938.

Appaloosas are light horses with beautiful spotted coats.

Today, there are about 350 different breeds. The breeds are divided into four basic groups: light, heavy (or draft), miniature or pony, and feral (or wild).

Light horses have small bones and thin legs. They weigh less than 1,300 pounds. Examples of light horses are Thoroughbreds, quarter horses, Morgan horses, and Appaloosas, or Appys. Appys are versatile and can be ridden over jumps or used to round up cattle. Appys are known for the dark spots on their coats.

Heavy horses, also known as draft horses, can weigh up to 2,000 or 3,000 pounds. They are strong with large bones and sturdy legs. Examples of heavy horses are Clydesdales and shire horses.

Draft horses are used on farms.

Miniature horses and ponies are shorter than other horses. Miniature horses are less than three feet tall. Ponies are usually not more than fifty-eight inches tall. Examples of breeds of ponies are Shetlands, Chincoteague, and the Canadian Pony of the Americas.

Feral horses are wild or semiwild. Semiwild means they live in the wild but are sometimes handled by people. The ancestors of today's feral horses escaped their owners or were released into the wild hundreds of years ago. Examples of feral horses are the mustang in North America, the brumby in Australia, and the Sorraia in Portugal.

Horses usually live for about twenty-five years but some live into their thirties and forties. With proper care, they will give their owners love and companionship for many years.

Chapter 3

The Right Horse for You

Horses are very expensive. But buying a horse is not the only cost of horse ownership. Before you buy one as a pet, talk with people who already own them. (Be careful when talking to someone who wants to sell you a horse.) Learn about the money, effort, and time you will spend when you become a horse owner. You should also learn how to ride horses and how to take care of them.

13

Volunteering at a horse rescue or riding stable is a good way to gain firsthand experience in caring for a horse.

The Right Horse for You

A great way to learn about horses is to volunteer at a horse rescue organization or a riding stable. You may also be able to lease a horse for six months, or you can share the care of a neighbor's horse.

Once you decide that you definitely want—and can take good care of—a horse, you need to choose one. There are hundreds of different breeds. Some breeds are better for certain activities. Do you want to participate in horse shows? Are you interested in trail riding? Do you want a pony or a retired horse that is happy to live in your pasture? Deciding what you are going to do with your pet will help you choose the right horse for you.

Fast ♘ Fact

Horses like to please their owners or trainers. Some have good memories and can be easily trained.

Rescue agencies work to find horses new homes.

Where Will You Get Your New Pet?

An experienced horse person can show you where to select a horse that matches your needs. You can also check with horse-rescue groups and humane societies that handle large animals. Many of these agencies rescue horses from owners that have hurt their horses. These agencies are willing to spend a lot of time finding good new homes for these horses. Be careful of horse auctions, bargains in the classified ads, and overeager horse dealers. If possible, find someone who knows a lot about horses to help you find the right one for you.

Pet ⏝ Pointer

Ask a horse expert questions before buying a horse.

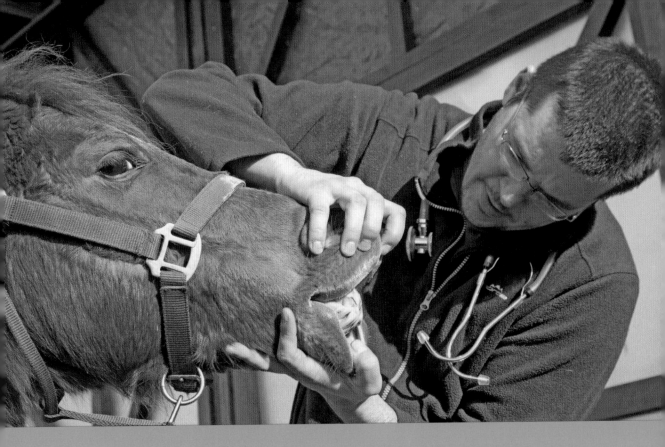

Before you buy a horse, have a veterinarian make sure it is healthy.

Once you have found a horse, ask a veterinarian, or animal doctor, to figure out the age and physical fitness of the horse. Remember not to make any decision based only on how the horse looks. Even beautiful horses can be unfit or bad tempered.

Chapter 4

Taking Care of Your Horse

Horses are very large and active animals. They need plenty of space to run and to rest. If you do not have space, you will need to board your horse at a stable or other boarding facility. Keeping a horse costs thousands of dollars a year. You will be spending that money on food, supplies, veterinary care, and emergencies.

A Comtois horse

Taking Care of Your Horse

If you board your horse, you will spend even more money. That is because you will be paying someone else to take care of your horse or renting space from them.

Your horse will generally stay healthiest and happiest in a large pasture with proper shelter available. There, it can graze, spend time with other horses, drink whenever it wants, and find protection from the weather as it chooses. As long as your horse has access to shelter, do not worry if it grazes in the rain or stands outside in the snow. Horses find shelter when they need it.

If you must keep your horse indoors for long periods, you will need to give it a stall or shed at least ten feet by ten feet, with access to an exercise area. The larger the space, the better. Place bedding in the stall, such as wood shavings or straw. What you choose depends on the cost and what is usually used where you live.

Taking care of a horse is a lot of work. You will need to take care of your pet every day, rain or shine. There are no holidays. You will need to buy grooming equipment, feed, buckets for feed and water, and feed storage barrels. If you plan to ride, you will also need a saddle, blanket, bridle or hackamore, lead rope, and halter.

Horses like to be outside. A corral is a closed-off area for holding animals.

Feeding

Horses basically need two types of feed: roughage, such as pasture grass and hay, and grain. Give your horse hay before you give it grain.

Horses need very specific amounts of food. Too much will make your horse fat, inactive, and even sick. Too little can make it weak and more likely to get sick.

Your horse's daily diet will depend on its breed, age, physical condition, and workload. Ask a vet or an expert on horse diets to help you choose a diet for your pet that is healthy but not too expensive. For more information check with experts at a county or state organization.

Fast ♘ Fact

A horse's stomach is small for the size of its body.

A horse eats pasture grass for roughage.

Taking Care of Your Horse

The most natural source of roughage is pasture grass. You can also give your horse one of several types of dry feed, such as hay. Good-quality hay, such as alfalfa, smells fresh and sweet. It is always green in color. Bad hay will be a gray, yellow, or brown color. It does not have much nutritional value. Also, bad hay can cause colic. This is a serious and sometimes fatal stomach illness in horses.

Stores carry a large selection of horse feeds, mixtures of several crushed grains, such as oats, corn, and barley. The grains are mixed with molasses. All grain should be clean and free of dust, bugs, mold, and musty smells.

Always set out a salt or mineral block for your horse. You can also give your pet apples, carrots, and store-bought treats as special rewards. Avoid sugar.

Feed your horse on a regular schedule. Feeding your pet three times a day is better than twice a day because a horse feels better when it eats frequent, small amounts. Overfeeding a hungry horse can cause it to get sick.

After a horse has finished eating, it should not be worked hard. Let your horse digest the meal. If you decide to change the type of feed you are giving your horse, do this slowly over seven days.

Always have clean water ready when your horse is in the corral or pasture.

watering

The amount of water your horse needs varies from five to twenty-five gallons a day, depending on how much water is in its feed, how much exercise your horse is getting, and how hot it is outside. Always give your horse some water before feeding it. Thirty minutes after your horse has finished eating, offer water again. In very cold weather, keep water buckets from freezing by breaking the ice several times a day or using a stock-tank heater.

After your horse has exercised, wait at least an hour before offering your pet water. You should never offer a horse water while it is hot unless it is working very hard, such as trail riding. Then, water your horse at every chance. Give your horse as much water as it wants, as long as it goes right back to work.

Never water a horse during work and then let your pet stand still. Your horse may get cramps and colic.

Grooming

Your new pet will need a lot of grooming. Groom your horse carefully before and after a day's work. Pay special attention to areas where saddles, girths, or bridles come in contact with its body. Crusty dirt may rub your horse and cause saddle sores.

To groom your horse, start at its head. Then, move to the left side of its neck. Groom all the way around the horse until you have groomed the entire body and legs.

Use a cloth to groom the horse's head. Over the rest of the body, use a rubber currycomb. Rub firmly and quickly in circle motions. This movement will massage the horse's skin and loosen dead hair and dirt.

Use special brushes to groom your horse.

Be sure to brush your horse's mane and tail.

Next, brush the horse's entire coat with a grooming brush. Make sure to brush in the same direction the hair grows.

Clean your horse's feet every day with a hoof pick. Look for nail punctures, rocks, wounds, and infections on the bottom of the feet.

Horses need shoes. They also need their hoofs trimmed. But it is best to leave the shoeing and hoof trimming to an expert called a farrier. A farrier will know how often to trim the hooves. Usually it is every two to three months.

You should also clean your horse's stall every day. You must scoop out the soiled or damp bedding and replace it with fresh bedding. If horses stand in damp bedding for too long, they can get a painful disease in their feet called thrush.

If you must sell your horse, carefully check out potential buyers. Make sure they want your horse as a pet. If you must part with an old or ill horse, do not sell it. It is best if your veterinarian euthanizes it, or puts it to death, with a painless shot at home.

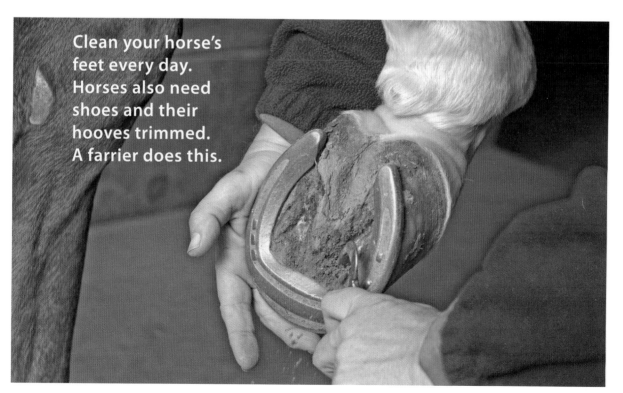

Clean your horse's feet every day. Horses also need shoes and their hooves trimmed. A farrier does this.

Chapter 5
Healthy and Happy

A veterinarian, often called a vet, takes care of sick and hurt animals. A vet also makes sure animals stay healthy. Horses have many ways of showing people they are sick. They may not eat, or they may limp. They may frequently paw the ground or kick at their stomach. They may lie down and not want to get up, or frequently try to roll over.

This baby horse is half Appaloosa and half Friesian.

Horses should be seen by a vet once a year for checkups.

If you see any signs of illness or injury in your horse, call the vet right away. Horses can get sick and die very quickly. Also, assemble a first-aid kit to have in case of an emergency. Your vet can tell you how to do this.

Horses can catch colds or come down with the flu. They can also get other, more serious diseases, such as tetanus and encephalitis or West Nile disease. These diseases can be prevented by vaccinations. Ask your vet what horse diseases are common in your area. Also ask how to recognize and prevent them.

Sometimes, you can see parasites on your horse such as flies, mosquitoes, and lice. Parasites can be controlled through proper cleaning as well as sprays. Some parasites, such as roundworm and bloodworm, are inside the horse's body. They cannot be seen. You may need to give your horse a medicine for these parasites.

Horses need a lot of exercise. If your horse is kept in a large pasture or very large pen, it may be able to create its own exercise by running, kicking up its heels, and chasing other horses. Otherwise, you must ride your horse or exercise it in some other way. Horses need to be exercised at least one hour a day. Longer is even better.

Horses need to be exercised every day. You can take lessons on how to properly ride your horse.

Some people may want to breed their horses. A baby horse is called a foal.

Some people want their horses to have babies. But breeding horses is very difficult and expensive. There are already too many baby horses being born that no one wants or that people cannot afford to care for.

If you do decide to breed your horse, you must have the money and time to properly care for the baby and the parents. You should ask a horse expert for help.

Chapter 6

Preventing Problems

Horses feel safe and happy around other horses. But, you may not be able to afford more than one horse. In this case, seek out chances for your horse to be around other horses, such as sharing a barn, stable, or pasture with someone else's horses.

You must make sure that the horses are watched until your horse gets to know the new horses.

Horses enjoy each other's company.

During feeding times, even gentle horses that know each other should be separated. That way, each horse will get its fair share.

Because of their size, horses can be dangerous. When they think they need to defend themselves, they bite and kick. People can become hurt badly or killed by a horse, no matter what size it is. To prevent problems, learn how to safely approach and handle horses from someone experienced. Know your pet's body language and sounds. That way, you will be able to interpret how your pet is feeling when you are spending time with it.

For example, horses say "hello" by blowing into each other's nose and face. Horses that are scared swish their tails and bare their teeth. Their ears become pinned back. Learn your horse's normal behavior so that you can tell when something is wrong.

Horses respond best to gentle training performed the same way each time. Any training that uses harsh equipment or pain is cruel. Horses are very smart and can learn to do many things, such as pull wagons or perform tricks. Some horse owners compete in horse shows.

People who own
horses can join
riding clubs and
compete in horse
shows.

Preventing Problems

Wild horses use their speed to save them from animals that might harm them. Domestic, or tame, horses still panic as a means of defense. They will try to outrun anything that scares them. When they are this way, they can easily hurt themselves. So be sure that stalls, gates, and fences do not have any sharp edges, nails that are sticking out, or broken boards.

Common objects in your horse's stall or pen may also cause accidents and injury. These items include pitchforks and buckets. Be sure to remove unnecessary items, and secure equipment to prevent your horse from getting hurt.

Keep dangerous objects away from your horse.

Preventing Problems

Any fence should be strong enough, visible enough, and high enough—about five feet—so your horse will not want to jump over it. Never use barbed wire to fence in a pasture. If you use another kind of wire, put the lowest strand at least two feet above the ground. Your horse is less likely to playfully stick a front leg over it.

Fences that surround pastures should be visible to your horse and high enough to keep it from jumping over.

Pet ♘ Pointer

Never tie your horse by its reins.
Use a lead rope instead.

Be sure the boards or rails in a horse's fence are close together. Otherwise, your horse may get its head stuck between them.

Never tie your pet to an object that could tear loose if the horse pulls back. Use an easily released slipknot to tie your horse.

If you believe a horse owner is neglecting, or failing to properly take care of, his or her pet, do not ignore the situation. Ask an adult to report it to the local humane society, animal control agency, or sheriff's department. If you think someone is abusing, or hurting, his or her horse, report this as well.

Chapter 7
You and Your New Horse

Horses need plenty of space. They have costly needs. They need a lot of their owners' time for feeding, grooming, and exercising. For all these reasons, horses are perhaps the most complicated pets to own. Remember that horses can live to be well over twenty years old. Keep loving and learning more about your pet, and you and your horse will spend many happy years together.

Enjoy taking care
of your new pet.

Life Cycle of a Horse

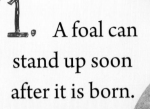

1. A foal can stand up soon after it is born.

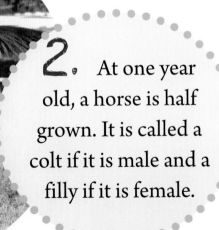

2. At one year old, a horse is half grown. It is called a colt if it is male and a filly if it is female.

3. Horses live for about twenty-five years, but some can live several years longer.

Words to Know

bridle—A harness to guide a horse's head.

colic—Severe pain in the stomach area.

currycomb—A comb shaped like a circle, with rows of teeth or ridges.

encephalitis—An illness that causes the brain to swell.

funeral procession—A ceremony where people follow the dead person's body to the cemetery.

girth—A measurement around something.

neglect—To fail to care properly for something.

pasture—An area of growing grass and other plants that animals can eat.

saddle—A seat for a rider on a horse.

tetanus—A disease that enters the body through a wound.

vaccination—A shot that prevents disease.

versatile—Able to do many different things.

West Nile disease—An illness that enters the body when an infected mosquito bites a person or animal.

Read More About Horses

Books

Crosby, Jeff, and Shelley Ann Jackson. *Harness Horses, Bucking Broncos, and Pit Ponies: A History of Horse Breeds.* Plattsburgh, N.Y.: Tundra Books, 2011.

Mack, Gail. *Horses.* Tarrytown, N.Y.: Marshall Cavendish Benchmark, 2010.

Wilsdon, Christine. *Horses.* Pleasantville, N.Y. : Gareth Stevens Pub., 2009.

Internet Addresses

American Humane Association
  <http://www.americanhumane.org/>

ASPCA: Horse Care
  <http://www.aspca.org/pet-care/horse-care/>

Index